THE FORGOTTEN THIRD:

DEVELOPING A BIBLICAL RELATIONSHIP WITH GOD THE HOLY SPIRIT

LARRY DIXON, PH.D.

I0149432

Energion Publications
Gonzalez, Florida
2022

Cover Art and Design: Jamie Lister

ISBN 978-1-63199-841-6
eISBN 978-1-63199-842-3
Library of Congress Control Number: 2022945110

Energion Publications
P. O. Box 841
Gonzalez, FL 32560

energion.com
pubs@energion.com

TABLE OF CONTENTS

INTRODUCTION

The Holy Spirit has been a special interest of mine for many years. I actually wrote my doctoral dissertation on Pneumatology (the doctrine of the Holy Spirit). It is entitled "The Pneumatology of John Nelson Darby (1800-1882)" and was completed at Drew University in 1985. Other than the dissertation committee, I think only my mother-in-law has read my dissertation. A pity.

I also had the privilege of writing a chapter with the title "The Other Comforter" for Dr. Jack Fish's book *Understanding the Trinity* (ECS Ministries, 2006). Not sure even my mother-in-law has read that chapter. But we keep writing.

I did not grow up in a charismatic or Pentecostal church, but I've always felt that those of us of a non-charismatic persuasion are missing something (or Someone) critical in life and theology.

I'm reminded of the story about a bank teller. The first man says, "I hear the First National Bank is looking for a new teller." The second man says, "I thought they just hired a new teller last week." The first man retorts, "Right. That's the one they're looking for." I believe some theological thievery has taken place — and we've missed out on much we need to know about God the Holy Spirit. So let's dive in!

I'm sure you've heard about the little boy who stops in front of a Catholic church with his bike and he sees the priest come out. The priest says, "Come inside, young man. I want to show you something very important about our faith."

The little boy says to the priest, "But somebody will steal my bike." The priest says to him, "Don't worry; the Holy Spirit will watch it."

So the little boy goes inside and the priest says, "Let me show you how to make the sign of the cross." The priest made the sign of the cross and said, "'In the name of the Father, the Son and the Holy Spirit, Amen.' Now you try it."

So the boy makes the sign of the cross and says, "In the name of the Father and the Son, Amen." The priest says, "What happened to the Holy Spirit?" The boy replied, "He's outside, watching my bike."

What a great question: "What happened to the Holy Spirit?" Some Christians act as if they have never heard of the Holy Spirit. It's true! They never talk about Him. They never refer to His work in their lives. It is as if He doesn't exist!

This is no new situation. In Acts 19 we read the following —

> While Apollos was at Corinth, Paul took the road through the interior and arrived at Ephesus. There he found some disciples [2] and asked them, "Did you receive the Holy Spirit when you believed?"
>
> They answered, "No, we have not even heard that there is a Holy Spirit."
>
> [3] So Paul asked, "Then what baptism did you receive?"
>
> "John's baptism," they replied.
>
> [4] Paul said, "John's baptism was a baptism of repentance. He told the people to believe in the one coming after him, that is, in Jesus." [5] On hearing this, they were baptized in the name of the Lord Jesus. [6] When Paul placed his hands on them, the Holy Spirit came on them, and they spoke in tongues and prophesied. [7] There were about twelve men in all.

These men, sometimes called the Ephesian Dozen, had not heard of God the Holy Spirit. It took the Apostle Paul's placing of his hands on them for the Holy Spirit to come on them and for that experience to be shown by their speaking in tongues and prophesying!

THE PROBLEM:

Now, I'm no Apostle Paul, but, it seems to me that many Christians today suffer from one or two serious errors about the

Holy Spirit. There are some who over**emphasize** Him and there are others who over**look** Him. We will challenge both of these errors, for we want a biblical balance in this critical topic.

The great spiritual writer A.W. Tozer put it this way:

> Our blunder (or shall we frankly say our sin?) has been to neglect the doctrine of the Spirit to a point where we virtually deny Him His place in the Godhead… The doctrine of the Holy Spirit as held by evangelical Christians today has almost no practical value at all.[1]

THE SOLUTION:

I will suggest that because the Holy Spirit is personal, we can (and should) develop a relationship with Him. We can speak to Him in prayer; we can ask Him for specific actions in our lives; we can treat Him as the Person He is! And because the Holy Spirit is divine, we can (and should) worship Him. But there is a caution with my "solution" which must be carefully considered.

As we will see, God the Holy Spirit has been sent to the church for a variety of reasons, not the least of which is that He would direct our attention to the Son of God, the Lord Jesus Christ. Some Christians have therefore concluded that the Third Person of the Trinity is not to receive any serious attention on our part, that He is always and rightly in the background,[2] and that to suggest a personal relationship with Him is simply theological error.

---

1   Essay entitled "A Costly Blunder" found at https://www.cmalliance.org/devotions/tozer?id=1489

2   It is interesting to note the many binitarian references (passages where the Father and the Son are mentioned, but not the Spirt) in the Scriptures, indicating (perhaps) the Spirit's behind-the-scenes role. See such texts as Mark 13:32; Romans 1:7; 1 Corinthians 1:3; 2 Corinthians 1:2; Galatians 1:3; Ephesians 1:2; Philippians 1:2; 2 Thessalonians 1:2; Philemon 3. See also Galatians 1:1; 1 Timothy 1:1; Titus 1:1; Ephesians 6:23; Philippians 2:11; 4:20, 23; Colossians 3:17; 1 Thessalonians 1:1; 3:11-13; etc.

This book will challenge that perspective as we examine His Person and His work in both the believer and non-believer.

CHAPTER I

A BIBLICAL BALANCE ON THE SPIRIT

Mike decided one week to analyze his prayers to the Lord. As he thought about his praying during devotions, his giving thanks at meal times, and his kind of SOS prayers during the day, he realized that most of his prayers were quite general. Often he prayed, "Father, please help me ..." Or, "Lord Jesus, I worship You for ..." He asked himself, *"Wait a minute! Is it ever right to pray to the Holy Spirit?"*

Great question, Mike! This kind of self-analysis is healthy, we believe, because it focuses the believer on the topic of prayer and the question "to whom should our prayers be directed?" Granted, it isn't a very well-thought-out prayer to pray, "Father, we thank You for dying on the cross for our sins," because it wasn't the Father who died for us! But how Person-specific ought we to be in our praying?

DIFFERENT MINISTRIES:

The doctrine of the Trinity is clear in the Bible (even if the term "Trinity" isn't used). The concept of the Trinity — Father, Son, and Holy Spirit — is specifically taught in the Word (Matthew 28; John 1). Each member of the Godhead is real and actively involved in the world and in the life of the follower of Jesus. The more we learn of God the Father the more we appreciate His care over creation (Psalm 19; Romans 14), His love in sending His Son (John 3:16), and His giving of the Spirit (1 Thessalonians 4:8 says He "give[s] His Spirit to those who ask Him").

The more we learn of God the Son, the Lord Jesus Christ, the more we love Him for His atoning work on the cross for us (Galatians 1:4; 2:20; Ephesians 5:2, 25; 1 Timothy 2:6; Titus 2:14.), for His abiding presence in our lives (Hebrews 13:5), and for the joy He wants us to have as we serve Him (John 17:13). Studying the ministries of the Son of God to us logically leads us to pray to Him in thanksgiving and praise.

But what about the Third Member of the Trinity? What about the Holy Spirit? What does He do? And are we right to pray to Him, to thank Him for what He does in our lives and in the world? Are we right to ask Him for things?

JESUS FIRST:

Let us be crystal clear that the Spirit of God was sent by the Father and the Son to glorify the Son, not Himself (John 16:12-14). There we read —

> [12] "I have much more to say to you, more than you can now bear. [13] But when he, the Spirit of truth, comes, he will guide you into all the truth. He will not speak on his own; he will speak only what he hears, and he will tell you what is yet to come. [14] He will glorify me because it is from me that he will receive what he will make known to you."

The Father declared in Isaiah 42:8, "My glory I will not share with another." And yet in John 17:5 Jesus prays, "And now, Father, glorify me in your presence with the glory I had with you before the world was." These two passages are a great proof of the deity of the Lord Jesus, right? God will not share His glory with idols. But we draw the wrong conclusion if we think that the Spirit of God is excluded from the glory of God.

We are to glorify the Father. And we are to glorify the Son. Are we to glorify the Spirit? Yes and No. No, in the sense that there is an order in the Trinity and the Spirit's primary role is to direct our attention to the Lord Jesus. But yes in the sense that we bring rightful glory to the Spirit when we become aware of and cooperate with His ministries in the world and in us — and when we praise Him for His work. Such honoring of the Spirit is not a detraction from the glory we give the Son.

The point is that there are ministries that are clearly done by the Holy Spirit — and we should acknowledge and cooperate with those ministries. We should be grateful to Him for what He does in our lives and in the world.

There is no mandate in the Bible that says we must "develop a relationship" with the Spirit of God. However, when I ask Him to bring conviction of sin to an unsaved friend, when I plead for His help in studying the Scriptures, or when I need to be reminded of my place in the family of God, these are aspects of a growing connection with God the Holy Spirit.

BIBLICAL EXAMPLES?

One might object and say, "There are no verses of any believers praying to God the Holy Spirit in the Bible!" And that person would be right. However, we might ask, are there any biblical examples of believers praying to the Son?

I would suggest that the account of Stephen's martyrdom in Acts 7 clearly shows Stephen praying to Jesus. We read, "While they were stoning him, Stephen prayed, 'Lord Jesus, receive my spirit.' Then he fell on his knees and cried out, 'Lord, do not hold this sin against them.' When he had said this, he fell asleep" (vv. 59-60).

That's the only example I can think of in which a believer prays directly to the Lord Jesus. But how many examples do we need? It is perfectly appropriate to pray to the Son of God.

But what about the Spirit of God? Can we — should we — pray to Him? Here believers often fall into two general categories: (1) those who will only do what Scripture clearly models and (2) those who feel free to do anything which the Scriptures do not prohibit.

Although we have no direct passages which show a believer praying specifically to the Third Person of the Trinity, I am suggesting we are free to do so. He is not to receive the primary attention of our lives. But to say that is not to say He should not receive any attention from us.

Our Jehovah's Witness friends deny the Trinity and say that the Holy Spirit is only God's active power. He is not personal, they say. In our next chapter we want to prove the personality of the Spirit — and draw certain conclusions based on that evidence.

STUDY QUESTIONS:

1. How would you present the doctrine of the Trinity from the Scriptures?

2. How would you prove from the Bible that the Spirit has been sent to glorify the Son?

3. Into what two categories can we divide Christians when it comes to a practice like praying to the Spirit?

CHAPTER 2

BECAUSE HE IS PERSONAL

I watched Bill and his son as they walked up my sidewalk. Bill was wearing a suit and carrying a leather briefcase. His son (probably about 8 years old) was also wearing a suit and carrying a little leather briefcase). I knew immediately that they were Jehovah's Witnesses.

I made a promise to the Lord years ago that I would no longer play Christian hide and seek when the cults came to my door. So, I stepped outside and greeted them, knowing that a good portion of my Saturday morning would be lost in theological debate.

As Bill and I talked, he shared with me what he believed as a Jehovah's Witness. They don't believe in blood transfusions; they don't salute the American flag; they reject the doctrine of the Trinity; they deny the personality and deity of the Holy Spirit.[3]

I listened carefully and then said to Bill, "Bill, there are a lot of areas we could discuss this morning. But wouldn't you agree that the most important issue is the Person of the Lord Jesus? Let's talk about who He is."

And so we did. For the next half an hour or so, he tried to convince me that Jesus was Michael the archangel who gave up his angelic nature to become human and to die on a torture stake as a sacrifice for my sins.

[I must tell you that we had to go over some ground rules before we began our discussion, for they are taught to

---

3   "God's holy spirit is not a God, not a member of a trinity, not coequal, and is not even a person ... It is God's active force ..." (Jehovah's Witnesses)

interrupt Christians and to control the conversation. One of the ground rules he agreed to was that we would not jump all over the Bible but stay with one passage until we agreed on its meaning or agreed to disagree. The other ground rule was that we would not interrupt each other. I had to remind him of this second ground rule a couple of times!]

Our conversation focused on the Person of the Lord Jesus. We could have discussed the Person of the Holy Spirit. And he would have told me that the Jehovah's Witnesses believe that the Spirit is not personal and that he is not divine and that he is not even a "he." The Spirit in their theology is God's mighty force. But we didn't discuss the Spirit.

I didn't feel I was getting very far in our discussion, although I tried to share the truth of Christ's deity with Bill several times. Finally, I sensed the Spirit's leading me to ask the following question: "Bill," I said, "is that your son?" The little boy had put his briefcase down and was playing with our dog in the front yard. "Yes," Bill said proudly. Bill was pleased that his son accompanied him in going door to door to share the Jehovah's Witnesses' "gospel."

"Bill," I said quietly, "you know that you and I can't both be right in our view of Jesus? You remember that Jesus said that whoever causes a little child who believes in Jesus to stumble deserves to have a large millstone hung around their neck and to be drowned in the depths of the sea, right?" I was referring to Matthew 18:6.

"Bill, I'm not sure how to say this, but if you are wrong in your view of the Lord Jesus, you are misleading your own son."

At that point Bill looked at his watch and said, "I'm sorry, but we have another appointment we've got to get to. Thanks for the conversation." And they left.

Bill and I could have talked at length about the Holy Spirit. But we didn't. That conversation was not the critical one.

However, is the Holy Spirit merely "Jehovah's impersonal force"? How do we know the Spirit is personal?

EVIDENCES OF PERSONALITY

Of course our Jehovah's Witness friends must reject the personality of the Holy Spirit because they reject the doctrine of the Trinity. They say the word "trinity" isn't in the Bible — and it isn't. But the concept of the Trinity is biblical. The term was coined by the Church Father Tertullian in the fourth century to account for the biblical material that God is both one and three. [There are many other terms that are not in the Bible, such as "theocracy" or "kingdom hall" or "Watchtower Tract and Bible Society."] Jehovah's Witnesses are, in my opinion, religious rationalists in the sense that what they can't understand they won't accept. They say it is illogical to think that $1+1+1 = 1$! [A rather juvenile retort by the Christian might be something like this: "Yes, but $1X1X1=1$! Right?"].

If my conversation partner Bill were to grant the personality of the Holy Spirit, he would have to admit that God is not mono-personal. And he would be fast on his way to affirming the doctrine of the Trinity!

By the way, it is interesting that the Greek word for "spirit" is neuter (Koiné Greek uses the three genders for nouns — masculine, feminine, and neuter), but He is routinely referred to as "He" in the Scriptures (see John 14-16 for Jesus' teaching on the Holy Spirit).

What evidences do we have that the Holy Spirit indeed is personal? Typically there are three characteristics that establish a personality: emotions, intellect, and will. In Scripture we have both didactic (teaching) and anecdotal evidence of the Spirit's personality. Didactically, Scripture tells us not to grieve the Holy Spirit (Ephesians 5:18- "Do not get drunk on wine, which leads to debauchery. Instead, be filled with the Spirit ..." See also Isaiah 63:10 where we read that Israel "rebelled and grieved his Holy Spirit. So he turned and became their enemy and he himself fought against them."). We grieve *persons*, do we not? Yes, we are to be filled with the Holy Spirit, but (as we'll see later) that involves being controlled and empowered by Him. Although we have no specific verse saying so, is it not logical that if we can grieve the Spirit, we can conversely bring joy to Him? We do, however, read in Galatians 6:8 that we can *please* the Spirit!

Romans 8 teaches that "Those who live according to the flesh have their minds set on what the flesh desires; but those who live in accordance with the Spirit have their minds set on what the Spirit desires. (v. 5). The Spirit has certain *desires* for us.

The intellect of God the Holy Spirit can be shown in several ways. Scripture is clear that the Holy Spirit leads the people of God — and it takes intelligence to do that. We read in Acts 13 the following —

> ² While they were worshiping the Lord and fasting, the Holy Spirit said, "Set apart for me Barnabas and Saul for the work to which I have called them."

The Spirit of God leads God's people (Romans 8:14 says, "For those who are led by the Spirit of God are the children of God."). The Spirit also reminds us of our adoption into God's family (Romans 8:16 says, "The Spirit himself testifies with our spirit that we are God's children."). The Spirit also desires to govern our minds, which assumes intellect (Romans 8:6 says, "The mind governed by the flesh is death, but the mind governed by the Spirit is life and peace.")

We frequently have the expression "the Spirit says …" Speaking takes intellect. Usually. The Spirit of God speaks (see 1 Corinthians 12:3; 1 Timothy 4:1 — "The Spirit clearly says that in later times some will abandon the faith …"; Hebrews 3:7; 10:15). We also have the recurring statement to the churches in the book of Revelation that they are to "hear *what the Spirit says* to the churches" (Revelation 2:7, 11, 17, 29; 3:6).

It also takes intelligence to *intercede* for others. Again we read in Romans 8 —

> ²⁶ In the same way, the Spirit helps us in our weakness. We do not know what we ought to pray for, but the Spirit himself intercedes for us through wordless groans. ²⁷ And he who searches our hearts knows the mind of the Spirit, because

the Spirit intercedes for God's people in accordance with the will of God.

We learn that the Holy Spirit is our primary *Teacher* in this dispensation — and His curriculum is the Word of God, the "sword of the Spirit" (Ephesians 6:17). Contrary to the opinion of some students, it takes intelligence to be a teacher!

Anecdotally, we also learn that the Spirit of God can be lied to (Acts 5, a text we will examine in our next chapter). We lie to persons, right?

The third evidence of the Spirit's personality is His will. The Spirit has a will — and that is to conform us to the image of the Lord Jesus. We saw in Acts 13 the Spirit's plan for an early missionary endeavor as He said, "Set apart for me Barnabas and Saul for the work to which I have called them." His *calling* indicates His will.

One aspect of His will for believers is expressed in Romans 8 — "For if you live according to the flesh, you will die; but if by the Spirit you put to death the misdeeds of the body, you will live." (v. 13). Part of His will is that the believer engage in the execution of the misdeeds of the body.

The Spirit gives spiritual gifts which are distributed according to His will (Hebrews 2:4). The issue of spiritual gifts will be examined more closely in Chapter 5.

Colossians 1:9 speaks of the Spirit's wisdom and understanding: "For this reason, since the day we heard about you, we have not stopped praying for you. We continually ask God to fill you with the knowledge of his will through all the wisdom and understanding that the Spirit gives …"

SUMMARY

If the Spirit of God is personal, then we can relate to Him. We can become concerned about His emotions and His responses to our behavior. We can seek to please Him, not lie to Him, nor grieve Him.

If we recognize the personality of God the Holy Spirit, we will clearly see that He is not God's impersonal force, but a Someone with whom we can develop a relationship. Developing that relationship, I would suggest, involves gaining a deeper understanding of His various ministries to the people of God.

STUDY QUESTIONS:

1. Given the little attention many Evangelicals pay to the Holy Spirit, aren't we almost like Jehovah's Witnesses in our treatment of Him? Why or why not?

2. List several emotions that you experience as a believer. Which might find a counterpart in the Holy Spirit?

3. How do we discover the **will** of the Holy Spirit?

CHAPTER 3

BECAUSE HE IS DIVINE[4]

"Are you telling me that the Holy Spirit is divine?", my Jehovah's Witness friend asked me. "Yes," I said. "He is not only personal, but He is the Third Person of the Trinity!" "How in the world would you prove that?", he asked. "Easy," I said. "Let me tell you a story."

But before we look at a fascinating — and frightening — story in the New Testament, let's think about God's "attributes." Theologians get paid by the big words and "attributes" is a big word meaning "characteristics." God has revealed certain truths about Himself in the Scriptures. His attributes include such characteristics as His mercy, holiness, justice, love, etc.

But typically there are three attributes (called the "omni's") that we need to consider. They are His omniscience, omnipotence, and omnipresence.

THE "OMNI'S" OF THE SPIRIT

If the Spirit of God is marked by these three "omni" attributes, then the logical conclusion is that He is God. Let's think about the Spirit's omniscience. For example, we read in 1 Corinthians 2 —

> The Spirit searches all things, even the deep things of God. [11] For who knows a person's thoughts except their own

---

4   An Explanatory Note: When we use the expression "The Forgotten Third" we are not suggesting that the Holy Spirit is 1/3 God. No, that would be heresy. He is fully God, just as are the Father and the Son. The term "Third" is referring to His Person in the Godhead, not His divinity.

spirit within them? In the same way no one knows the thoughts of God except the Spirit of God.

We also read in 1 John 2 —

> [20] But you have an anointing from the Holy One, and all of you know the truth. [21] I do not write to you because you do not know the truth, but because you do know it and because no lie comes from the truth.

And the Lord Jesus promises His disciples in John 14 the following: "But the Advocate, the Holy Spirit, whom the Father will send in my name, will teach you all things and will remind you of everything I have said to you." (v. 26).

All the many verses in Scripture that speak of God's omniscience have application to the Third Member of the Godhead who is divine.

Let's continue and consider the Spirit's omnipotence. By this term we mean His all-powerfulness. God can do all that is consistent with His own nature. Scripture tells us that God cannot lie ("it is impossible for God to lie," says Hebrews 6:18). We read in Titus 1:2 about "God, who does not lie ..." 2 Timothy 2:13 tells us that God can't deny Himself.

The Spirit's power is shown in Luke 1 where the angel Gabriel explains to Mary about the Christ-child: "The angel answered, "The Holy Spirit will come on you, and the power of the Most High will overshadow you. So the holy one to be born will be called the Son of God." (v. 35; see also Romans 15:19 regarding the Spirit's power). The Spirit of God caused the biological process (involving a male) to be circumvented as Mary becomes pregnant without any help from Joseph.

Let's think about the Spirit's attribute of omnipresence. I like how the theologian Millard Erickson explains this attribute: "Wherever there's a 'where,' God is there!" God is not spatially limited in any way. In fact we read in Psalm 139 —

> Where can I go from your Spirit?
> Where can I flee from your presence?
> [8] If I go up to the heavens, you are there;
> if I make my bed in the depths, you are there.

If, indeed, the Spirit of God *indwells* the believer (as we will see in a subsequent chapter), the child of God is never alone. Never abandoned. He or she has the Spirit of God living in them! And He has promised never to leave us (we read in John 14:16-17- "And I will ask the Father, and he will give you another advocate to help you and be with you forever— the Spirit of truth.").

The Spirit of God displays the three characteristics of deity — omniscience, omnipotence, and omnipresence.

ANECDOTAL EVIDENCE

Although there are other evidences of the deity of the Holy Spirit, my favorite comes from Acts 5. There we read of a couple (Ananias and Sapphira) who apparently wanted to be like Barnabas who donated money to the apostles (in Acts 4:36-37). But they really didn't want to give their all to the Lord, so they sold a piece of property and lied about its sale price. Let's hear the text itself:

> Then Peter said, "Ananias, how is it that Satan has so filled your heart that you have lied to the Holy Spirit and have kept for yourself some of the money you received for the land? Didn't it belong to you before it was sold? And after it was sold, wasn't the money at your disposal? What made you think of doing such a thing? You have not lied to men but to God." (Acts 5:3-4)

Please notice several important factors here. Ananias and Sapphira were not forced into selling their property. We are not talking about some kind of communism in this event. They were free to sell it or not sell it. And they were free to keep the proceeds after the sale of the property. What they were not free to do was to lie to the Holy Spirit! And Peter makes the point that they had not deceived or lied only to the early church. They had not lied only to men but to God! And the text makes it crystal clear that LYING TO THE HOLY SPIRIT = LYING TO GOD! That's our point here in Acts 5, that the Holy Spirit is clearly called "God."

But the story is too good to stop at verse 4. The moment Ananias heard the words, "You have not lied to men but to God," he kicked the bucket! The youth group came and buried the body (allow me a little liberty here). And then Sapphira showed up.

One wonders where she had been. The text tells us that it is about three hours after her husband had died (v. 7). Some have suggested that, because she had money in her pocket and time on her hands, she was out shopping — but the Bible doesn't tell us that.

At any rate, Peter asks her a straightforward question: "Tell me, is this the price you and Ananias got for the land?" (v. 8) Let's say that they sold the land for $100, but gave the apostles only $75 (proclaiming that they had gotten exactly $75 for the land). Peter's question essentially is: "Did you and your husband really sell the land for $75?" Don't miss this point! God gives Sapphira an opportunity to "come clean." She is not being judged for her husband's sin. She seeks to perpetuate the ruse when she replies, "Yes, that is exactly what we got for the land!" The last words she hears are: "How could you agree to test the Spirit of the Lord? Look! The feet of the men who buried your husband are at the door, and they will carry you out also" (v. 9). And the youth group gets to take another sad field trip to the local cemetery.

The late, great preacher Vance Havner commented on this passage. He said, "Isn't it good that God does not act in such judgment today? If He did, every church would need a morgue in its basement!"[5]

STUDY QUESTIONS:

1. How should we qualify our statement that "God can do all things"?

---

5   Some of the preceding section was taken from our book *DocTALK: A Fairly Serious Survey of All That Theological Stuff* (Christian Focus, 2001).

2. What is your personal takeaway from the story of Ananias and Sapphira?

3. Why did God act with such dramatic judgment in Acts 5?

CHAPTER 4

HIS MINISTRIES TO THE BELIEVER (PART 1)

"My friend Mike seems to have no sense of his own sin, no awareness that he is lost before a thrice-holy God. How can I help him?", Susan asked. My answer was quite simple: "We need to study the Spirit of God and avail ourselves of His various activities in the world, in the believer — and in the unbeliever."

While some believers over**emphasize** the Person of the Holy Spirit, many over**look** Him and His many ministries in the world. We want a biblical balance as we study the Third Person of the Trinity.

As I study the Scriptures, I find over twelve ministries of the Holy Spirit in the life of the Jesus-follower. We will look at three of those ministries (and one of His titles) in this chapter.

(1) THE INDWELLING OF THE HOLY SPIRIT

Scripture is clear that when a person trusts Christ he or she is immediately *indwelt* by the Spirit of God. We read in 1 Corinthians 3 —

> [16] Don't you know that you yourselves are God's temple and that God's Spirit dwells in your midst? [17] If anyone destroys God's temple, God will destroy that person; for God's temple is sacred, and you together are that temple.

We also read in 1 Corinthians 6 —

[18] Flee from sexual immorality. All other sins a person commits are outside the body, but whoever sins sexually, sins against their own body. [19] Do you not know that your bodies are temples of the Holy Spirit, who is in you, whom you have received from God? You are not your own; [20] you were bought at a price. Therefore honor God with your bodies.

What are the implications of having the Spirit of God indwell us? From these two texts in 1 Corinthians, it is clear that God cares about our bodies. We are not to destroy what God has given to us. We are also reminded that we don't belong to ourselves! We've been bought with a price — and we are to therefore honor God with our bodies which are the temples of the Holy Spirit.

(2) THE BAPTISM OF THE SPIRIT/THE NEW BIRTH

One of the more debated ministries of the Spirit of God is His work of baptizing us into the body of Christ. Acts 2, many Evangelicals believe, is the beginning of the Church and the baptism of the Holy Spirit is the theological explanation of what takes place there at Pentecost. I think that a careful examination of Acts, chapters 2, 10, and 11, as well as 1 Corinthians 12:13 indicate that the baptism of the Spirit occurs when one is converted and it is the action by which the Spirit incorporates a new believer into the body of Christ.

The baptizing work of the Spirit is when He brings us into the family of God. We read in 1 Corinthians 12:13 — "For we were all baptized by one Spirit so as to form one body—whether Jews or Gentiles, slave or free—and we were all given the one Spirit to drink."

Luke writes the following in Acts 1 —

[4] On one occasion, while he was eating with them, he gave them this command: "Do not leave Jerusalem, but wait for the gift my Father promised, which you have heard me speak about. [5] For John baptized with water, but in a few days you will be baptized with the Holy Spirit."

It is easy to confuse water baptism with the baptism of the Holy Spirit. We read, for example, in the book of Acts —

> Then I remembered what the Lord had said: 'John baptized with water, but you will be baptized with the Holy Spirit.' (11:16),

And in Romans Paul writes —

> Or don't you know that all of us who were baptized into Christ Jesus were baptized into his death? (6:3)

Water baptism is clearly referred to in such passages as the following —

> Peter replied, "Repent and be **baptized**, every one of you, in the name of Jesus Christ for the forgiveness of your sins. And you will receive the gift of the Holy Spirit. (Acts 2:38)

Those who accepted his message were **baptized**, and about three thousand were added to their number that day. (Acts 2:41)

> As they traveled along the road, they came to some water and the eunuch said, "Look, here is water. What can stand in the way of my being **baptized**?" (Acts 8:36)
> And he gave orders to stop the chariot. Then both Philip and the eunuch went down into the water and Philip **baptized** him. (Acts 8:38)

I don't know of any verses that declare that water baptism brings about the baptism of the Spirit, or that water baptism is required for one to receive the baptism of the Spirit. It seems to me that one does not pray for this ministry of the Spirit, but that the Spirit sovereignly performs this action upon a person's conversion.

The primary text on **the new birth** is John 3 of course. There we read about the Spirit's work in bringing one into the kingdom of God. One must be "born of water and the Spirit" (v. 5), probably indicating physical followed by spiritual birth. The Spirit is the One who "gives birth to spirit" (v. 6). And the Spirit's work is like the wind: it is unpredictable. Jesus says, "so it is with everyone born of the Spirit" (v. 8). The one who believes in the Son of Man "may have eternal life in him" (v. 15), "shall not perish" (v. 16), and will not be condemned (v. 18).

There are other references in the New Testament about being born of the Spirit (1 Peter 1:23). The one who doesn't "have" the Spirit of Christ does not belong to Christ, we learn in Romans 8:9. It is the Spirit of God who lives in the believer and gives life to our mortal bodies, according to Romans 8:11. Upon conversion we are no longer our own; we are bought at a price and become the temples of the Holy Spirit (1 Corinthians 6:19-20).

(3) THE OTHER COMFORTER

[Some of the following was originally presented in an academic conference and is a bit technical]:

Jesus refers to the Holy Spirit as "another Comforter" in John 14:16, and simply as "the Comforter" in John 14:26, 15:26, and 16:7 (KJV). In those contexts He also refers to the Spirit three times as "the Spirit of truth" (in John 14:17, 15:26, and 16:13), once as "the Holy Spirit" (in John 14:26), and once simply as "the Spirit" (in John 16:15). All of these titles are worthy of serious contemplation, but we want to focus on the specific expression, "another Comforter."

The Greek expression is simply *allos parakletos* – an adjective followed by another adjective (a substantive). The term *allos* carries the idea of "another of the same kind." Jesus does not use the adjective *heteros* which would carry the implication "another of a different kind." The commentator Swete says that the Spirit is "a second of the same and not of a different order."

The expression "another" Comforter raises the question "Other than what/whom?" One commentator argues that since Christ did not refer to Himself as a *paracletos*, He might mean "one other than yourselves," that is, "another Spirit like yours but beyond yours." But it must be pointed out that although Christ did not use the term paraclete of Himself, He did speak of performing actions which a Paraclete might well perform.

The traditional translation of the phrase as "another Comforter" has met strong opposition, especially from the scholar Samuel Chadwick. He writes,

> It is deplorable that our English version mistranslates the Greek *Paraclete* by the word *Comforter*. Jesus did not promise another Comforter, but another Paraclete... It is impossible to read the four passages in which the word occurs without feeling the inadequateness of Comforter for the office He fills. Instruction, witnessing, and conviction are not usually associated with the ministry of consolation. The translation entirely misses the mark, and is responsible for untold mischief in both doctrine and experience; and yet it has prevailed from the days of the Fathers to the latest version of the Scriptures. It misrepresents the Mission of the Spirit, has led believers to think less of obligation than of comfort, and has associated Christianity with soothing consolations rather than with conflict. The need is not comfort, but power. The call is not to pampered softness, but to the hardship of service and the strain of battle. The Holy Spirit is not given to be a nursing mother to fretful children, but the captain of a mighty host full of nerve and fire.

The New Testament scholar D.A. Carson wryly says, "In today's ears, 'Comforter' sounds either like a quilt or like a do-gooder at a wake, and for most speakers of English should be abandoned. 'Helper' (GNB) is not bad, but has overtones of being subordinate or inferior, overtones clearly absent from John 14-16."

Although Jesus did not use the term paraclete of Himself, it must not be forgotten that He is indeed called our paraclete in I John 2:1. The NIV translates that verse as "... But if anybody does sin, we have one who speaks to the Father in our defense – Jesus Christ, the Righteous One." Six words are needed in English ("one who speaks ... in our defense") to translate the simple term paraclete. And in the context of I John 2, the need is not comfort, but defense for the believer who has sinned.

Another commentator, Beasley-Murray, compares the Holy Spirit and Jesus in light of this use of paraclete for Jesus in I John 2:

> Here Jesus is depicted as an intercessor *in* the court of heaven, representing the cause of his own, whereas the Holy Spirit is the Paraclete *from* heaven, supporting his own in the face of a hostile world. The ministries of the two Paracletes, however, are thought of not as *simultaneous*, but as successive. The Spirit-Paraclete takes the place of the Paraclete Jesus after Jesus' departure to the Father.

Although the term paraclete is explicitly used only once of the Lord Jesus, by implication John 14:16 should also be considered a reference to Jesus as paraclete ("another Comforter"). Because the logical meaning is that the Spirit would be to the disciples as Jesus was to them, there are a number of implications which we will notice momentarily.

The term *parakletos* has generated much discussion concerning its definition. Being passive in form it has the literal meaning of "called to the side of." Morris points out that "As a substantive it was used (though not often), like its Latin equivalent *advocatus*, as a legal term indicating the counsel for the defense." Therefore it could be defined as "called to one's aid, in a court of justice."

However, "Advocate" might not be the best translation in all contexts. When the Spirit engages in activities like arguing and instructing, these are not necessarily actions associated with an Advocate. One commentator points out that "Such a person would certainly argue, but on behalf of his client. He would instruct, but not the client. He would instruct the court. In John the *paracletos* is found instructing those whose *paracletos* He is." In short, *paracletos* "as the Greeks knew this legal functionary was not as precisely defined as our counsel for the defence."

John Wycliffe gets the credit or blame for the translation "Comforter," according to Leon Morris. "Comforter" can be defended as a translation if the English word is taken in its etymological sense (Latin, *con*, "with" and *fortis*, "strong"). It will then have the implication of "Strengthener" or "Helper."

But in modern times "comfort" has come to have a meaning like "consolation." It points to a making the best of a difficult situation, whereas the idea in *paracletos* is not so much this as that of providing the assistance that will deliver from the difficult situation. "Helper" is rather better, but it does not really face the fact that the word is not active in meaning.

C.K. Williams opts for the translation "Friend." Others suggest especially a legal friend. Knox has renderings like "another to befriend you." Morris points out that "It seems that it is something like this that is needed, though the legal background of the term is not to be overlooked. John is thinking of the Friend at court ..."

Morris concludes the discussion on the meaning of Paraclete by writing,

> The One who stands for us as the Friend at the heavenly court will perform functions that would not be required in any earthly court. Thus He will remind us of what Christ has said (14: 26). For heavenly purposes in certain circumstances this may well be the most important thing that can be done. So with His teaching of us, of His bearing witness to Christ, His convicting of the world, and the rest. In all these things He is the legal helper, the friend who does whatever is necessary to forward their best interests. But it is impossible to find one English word that will cover all that the *paracletos* does. We must content ourselves with a term which stresses a limited aspect or aspects, or else use such a term as "Paraclete."

IMPLICATIONS OF OUR "OTHER COMFORTER"

R. E. Brown provides a helpful summary when he writes that

> [T]he Paraclete is a *witness* in defence of Jesus and a *spokesman* for him in the context of the trial of Jesus by his enemies; the Paraclete is a *consoler* of the disciples; more important, he is their teacher and guide and thus, in an extended sense, their *helper*. No one translation captures the complexity of these functions ... Christian usage has given a peculiar connotation and status to *[paracletos]* – a connotation not entirely inde-

pendent of related Hebrew concepts and of the secular Greek meaning of the words, – but a connotation that is unique just the same.

Jesus says the Holy Spirit would be "another *paraclete*" to His disciples. Would the term "comfort" be the first to come to mind when we think of how Jesus was to His disciples? He rebukes them for their unbelief, for their sleeping, for having no faith. He defends them when they are accused of violating sacred rules of ceremonial washing or ignoring Sabbath observance. He "comes alongside" them when their faith is too weak to exorcize a demon-possessed boy.

"Comfort" seems to imply bringing solace to one who is weeping. The disciples (during the earthly ministry of the Lord) did not know enough to weep. He does not "comfort" them – He challenges, chastises, corrects, and even cajoles them. "Comfort" is far too weak a term. And sometimes the last thing the believer needs is a sympathetic companion who wipes away his tears. We need One who is fully divine to come alongside of us and put His finger on our sins and remind our hearts, "You belong to Your Heavenly Father." We require One who will motivate and empower us to take risks for the Kingdom of God, One who will not be satisfied with one-seventh of our week, with the leftovers of our hours and days. We need One who will be "called alongside of" us even when we ourselves don't have enough wisdom to invite His intrusive presence.

In an age of comfort food, we need the Bread of Life broken to us by the Spirit who yearns for our sanctification. We desperately require a Defender in the face of undeserved, snarling rebukes by an unbelieving world – and in the face of deserved charges of our sins by the great Accuser, Satan himself. The Spirit is not a soothing Teddy Bear, but the Hound of Heaven who will not let us be.

Our primary need is not for Someone who will say, "There, there. It will all be okay. It really doesn't matter." We require Someone who will remind us that life matters greatly, that we might well die for the sake of the gospel – and we are no fools if such happens to us. We need Someone who will remind us of our son-ship even when Satan, the world around us, other Christians, and even our own conduct seem to contradict the very idea that we could be loved and forgiven by God. We need to be *rescued* from our consumeristic culture and transformed into God-centered, other-focused ambassadors for the King. In our postmodern atmosphere where it seems no one knows who they are and have stopped asking such questions, the Spirit reminds us of our adoption into God's family. In our subjective circles of pooled ignorance, often punctuated by "Here's what the Lord says to me," we need the determined Applier of the truth of Scripture to do His mighty work in conjunction with the serious attention to the meaning of the Word. Surrounded by moral relativity and a resistance to anyone who defends the concepts of right and wrong, we desperately need the inner conviction of the Spirit who does not debate moral matters with us but puts His divine finger on the shortcomings of our thoughts and actions. In brief, we need Someone like Jesus.[6]

STUDY QUESTIONS:

1. How are we to understand the baptism of the Holy Spirit?

2. How is "Comforter" not necessarily a good translation of paracletos?

3. How does the ministry of the Spirit differ from the ministry of Christ, do you think?

---

6   The above material on "The Other Comforter" is from my book *DocTALK: A Fairly Serious Survey of All That Theological Stuff* (Christian Focus, 2001).

CHAPTER 5

HIS MINISTRIES TO THE BELIEVER (PART 2)

"I don't know what God wants me to do in the local church!", my friend Ismael said. "How am I supposed to serve? Where am I supposed to serve?" "May I ask you," I said, "what are your spiritual gifts?" Ismael said, "I have no clue!"

Before we analyze the passages on spiritual gifts, let's think about the Holy Spirit's ministry of teaching and filling.

(1) THE TEACHING MINISTRY OF THE HOLY SPIRIT

We have a wonderful section called "the Upper Room Discourse" in which Jesus gives us much information about God the Holy Spirit (John 14-16). We learn a great deal about Jesus' sending the Spirit as His replacement and as our Teacher.

We see in **John 14** that the Holy Spirit is a gift to the disciples, requested of the Father by the Son (14:16). He comes to help and to indwell Jesus' followers (14:16) as the Spirit of truth (14:17). He is the manifestation of the absent Christ to them (14:18) so that they will not be orphans. Sent from the Father, the Holy Spirit, the Advocate, will teach the disciples all things and will remind them of all Jesus had taught them (14:26).

In **John 15** we learn that the Spirit of truth whom Jesus will send from the Father will testify about Christ (15:26). That is His curriculum. And the disciples are to pass on that testimony (15:27).

John 16 has the most information about the Spirit of God and the disciples. We learn —

1. It is for the disciples' benefit that Jesus is going back to the Father, for "unless I go away, the Advocate will not come to you" (16:7). The Holy Spirit's presence necessitated Jesus' absence.

2. The Spirit's work will be that of proving the world wrong! The world is wrong regarding sin and righteousness and judgment (16:8). Each of these areas is explained: the world is wrong about sin because people don't believe in Jesus; about righteousness because He is going to the Father where the disciples can see Him no longer; about judgment because the prince of this world now stands condemned (16:9-11).

3. The Spirit's guidance is promised — "He will guide you into all the truth" 16:12). He won't speak on His own but will only speaks what He hears and will tell you what is yet to come (16:13). There is an on-going communication between the members of the Trinity.

4. We learn that the Spirit's role is to glorify the Son (16:14). Jesus says, "He will glorify me because it is from me that he will receive what he will make known to you" (16:14).

(2) THE FILLING MINISTRY OF THE HOLY SPIRIT

We have seen that even though some refer to the Spirit as the "Shy Member of the Trinity," this does not negate the fact that because He is a Person we can have a relationship with Him. And because He is God, we can and should worship Him. We've noticed His indwelling ministry. As the "other Comforter" (or "Advocate"), the Spirit of God comes alongside us to help us or to put His divine finger on something in our lives that needs to change. We've also learned that He has a teaching ministry to the believer. What else does Scripture teach us about the many ministries that the Holy Spirit has to the follower of Jesus?

We learn that He fills the believer. There are many verses in the book of Acts showing the Spirit's filling of the early Christians:

Acts 2:4
All of them were filled with the Holy Spirit and began to speak in other tongues as the Spirit enabled them.

Acts 4:8
Then Peter, filled with the Holy Spirit, said to them: "Rulers and elders of the people!"

Acts 4:31
After they prayed, the place where they were meeting was shaken. And they were all filled with the Holy Spirit and spoke the word of God boldly.

Acts 9:17
Then Ananias went to the house and entered it. Placing his hands on Saul, he said, "Brother Saul, the Lord— Jesus, who appeared to you on the road as you were coming here—has sent me so that you may see again and be filled with the Holy Spirit."

Acts 13:9
Then Saul, who was also called Paul, filled with the Holy Spirit, looked straight at Elymas and said,

Acts 13:52
And the disciples were filled with joy and with the Holy Spirit.

While the filling of the Spirit on the day of Pentecost was unique, the Bible does not teach that all believers should speak in other tongues (1 Corinthians 12:30).

In our other passages we learn that the Holy Spirit's filling enables believers to speak clearly before those in authority (Acts 4:8) and with boldness (Acts 4:31; 13:9).

Frequently being filled with the Spirit is coupled with another characteristic (joy, Acts 13:52; wisdom, Acts 6:3; faith, Acts 6:5: 11:24; God's grace and power, Acts 6:8, power to die, Acts 7:55).

Ephesians 5:18 says, "Do not get drunk on wine, which leads to debauchery. Instead, be filled with the Spirit." We are commanded to be filled with the Spirit. It is interesting that this verse (including the verses above) doesn't tell the believer how to be filled with the Spirit.

In his article entitled "How to Be Filled with the Spirit," Pastor John Piper suggests what he calls the closest parallel: "Don't be drunk with wine; be filled with the Spirit (Ephesians 5:18). How do you get drunk with wine? You drink it. Lots of it. The wine of Paul's day was so weak you would have to drink for hours to get drunk. So how then shall we get drunk (filled) with the Spirit? Drink it! Lots of it. Paul said in 1 Corinthians 12:13, 'We were all ... made to drink of one Spirit.' Jesus said, 'If anyone thirsts, let him come to me and drink. Whoever believes in me, as the Scripture has said, 'Out of his heart will flow rivers of living water.' Then John writes, 'Now this he said about the Spirit.' (John 7:37-39)."

How do you drink of the Spirit? You set your mind on the things of the Spirit (Romans 8:5). We set our minds on things above (Colossians 3:1-2). "So drinking the Spirit means seeking the things of the Spirit, directing your attention to the things of the Spirit, being devoted to the things of the Spirit."

The things of the Spirit refers to the teachings of the apostles about God and to the words of Jesus. Doing this long enough will get us drunk with the Spirit. We will develop a wonderful Spirit-dependency.

Lastly, Piper says, "The Holy Spirit is not like wine because he is a person and is free to come and go where he wills (John 3:8). Therefore Luke 11:13 must be added. Jesus said to his disciples, "If you then, who are evil, know how to give good gifts to your children, how much more will the heavenly Father give the Holy Spirit to those who ask him!" If we want to be filled with the Spirit, we must pray for it. And that is just what Paul does for the Ephesians in 3:19. He asks his Father in heaven (verse 14) that the believers might be "filled with all the fullness of God." Drink and pray. Drink and pray. Drink and pray."[7]

(3) THE GIFTS OF THE HOLY SPIRIT

There is so much to be done in the local church! How are the various "ministries" supposed to get accomplished?

God in His brilliance equips the people of God to do the work of God. And His equipping of the saints is called the gifts of the Holy Spirit.

Every believer in Christ has been gifted with some talent or ability to build up the Body of Christ. Four key passages speak about those gifts — and the sovereign Holy Spirit who distributes those gifts (Romans 12, 1 Corinthians 12, Ephesians 4, and 1 Peter 4). We will briefly look at each of those four primary texts and draw certain conclusions about this work of the Third Person of the Trinity.

Let's take a brief look at Romans 12 —

> Therefore, I urge you, brothers and sisters, in view of God's mercy, to offer your bodies as a living sacrifice, holy and pleasing to God—this is your true and proper worship. ² Do not conform to the pattern of this world but be transformed by the renewing of your mind. Then you will be able to test and approve what God's will is—his good, pleasing and perfect will. ³ For by the grace given me I say to every one of you: Do not think of yourself more highly than you ought, but rather think of yourself with sober judgment, in accordance with the faith God has distributed to each of you. ⁴ For just as each of us has one body with many members, and these members do not all have the same function, ⁵ so in Christ we, though many, form one body, and each member belongs to all the others.

7   https://www.desiringgod.org/articles/how-to-be-filled-with-the-spirit

⁶ We have different gifts, according to the grace given to each of us. If your gift is prophesying, then prophesy in accordance with your faith; ⁷ if it is serving, then serve; if it is teaching, then teach; ⁸ if it is to encourage, then give encouragement; if it is giving, then give generously; if it is to lead, do it diligently; if it is to show mercy, do it cheerfully.

Notice here in Romans 12 the following —

1. We should view our bodies as living sacrifices to God, the very definition of "true and proper worship" (v. 1).

2. We must be aware that the world around us wants to squeeze us into its mold, but we need the transforming work of God to renew our minds (v. 2).

3. Choosing to transform rather than conform means that we will be able to test and approve what God's will is for us (v. 2).

4. Our attitude in using our gifts is critical! We are to look at ourselves with "sober judgment," being mindful of "the faith" which God has distributed to each of us (v. 3).

5. In Christ we are one body with many members. And those members (who belong to each other) have different functions (vv. 4-5).

6. Different gifts according to the grace given to us include: prophesying, serving, teaching, encouraging, giving, leading, and showing mercy (vv. 6-8).

7. We are to use those gifts "in accordance with our faith." We are to give generously, lead diligently, and show mercy cheerfully (vv. 6-8).

What do we learn about the Spirit and the gifts in 1 Corinthians 12?

⁴ There are different kinds of gifts, but the same Spirit distributes them. ⁵ There are different kinds of service, but the same Lord. ⁶ There are different kinds of working, but in all of them and in everyone it is the same God at work. ⁷ Now to each one the manifestation of the Spirit is given for the common good. ⁸ To one there is given through the Spirit a

message of wisdom, to another a message of knowledge by means of the same Spirit, [9] to another faith by the same Spirit, to another gifts of healing by that one Spirit, [10] to another miraculous powers, to another prophecy, to another distinguishing between spirits, to another speaking in different kinds of tongues, and to still another the interpretation of tongues. [11] All these are the work of one and the same Spirit, and he distributes them to each one, just as he determines.

[12] Just as a body, though one, has many parts, but all its many parts form one body, so it is with Christ. [13] For we were all baptized by one Spirit so as to form one body—whether Jews or Gentiles, slave or free—and we were all given the one Spirit to drink. [14] Even so the body is not made up of one part but of many.

[15] Now if the foot should say, "Because I am not a hand, I do not belong to the body," it would not for that reason stop being part of the body. [16] And if the ear should say, "Because I am not an eye, I do not belong to the body," it would not for that reason stop being part of the body. [17] If the whole body were an eye, where would the sense of hearing be? If the whole body were an ear, where would the sense of smell be? [18] But in fact God has placed the parts in the body, every one of them, just as he wanted them to be. [19] If they were all one part, where would the body be? [20] As it is, there are many parts, but one body.

[21] The eye cannot say to the hand, "I don't need you!" And the head cannot say to the feet, "I don't need you!" [22] On the contrary, those parts of the body that seem to be weaker are indispensable, [23] and the parts that we think are less honorable we treat with special honor. And the parts that are unpresentable are treated with special modesty, [24] while our presentable parts need no special treatment. But God has put the body together, giving greater honor to the parts that lacked it, [25] so that there should be no division in the body, but that its parts should have equal concern for each other. [26] If one part suffers, every part suffers with it; if one part is honored, every part rejoices with it.

²⁷ Now you are the body of Christ, and each one of you is a part of it. ²⁸ And God has placed in the church first of all apostles, second prophets, third teachers, then miracles, then gifts of healing, of helping, of guidance, and of different kinds of tongues. ²⁹ Are all apostles? Are all prophets? Are all teachers? Do all work miracles? ³⁰ Do all have gifts of healing? Do all speak in tongues? Do all interpret? ³¹ Now eagerly desire the greater gifts.

We realize that this is a lengthy passage, but let's see what we can learn, not so much about the gifts, but about the Giver, God the Holy Spirit:

1. First of all, it is He who distributes the gifts (v. 4).

2. Although there are different gifts, the same Lord is at work (v. 6).

3. Every believer is given a gift (also known as a "manifestation of the Spirit") for the common good (v. 7).

4. Several gifts (nine specifically) are listed (vv. 8-10- a message of wisdom, a message of knowledge, faith, gifts of healing, miraculous powers, prophecy, distinguishing between spirits, speaking in different kinds of tongues, the interpretation of tongues). But the point is made that "all these are the work of one and the same Spirit" (vv. 11). The oneness of the Spirit's distribution is important here.

5. We also learn of His will — He distributes these gifts "just as He determines" (v. 11).

6. The baptizing work of the Spirit is brought up, presumably to emphasize the oneness of the Body of Christ (v. 12). "We were all given the one Spirit to drink" (v. 13).

7. There is no room for jealousy regarding the gifts or for one to feel unnecessary. Why not? Because we need all the body parts to function properly and "God has placed the parts in the body, every one of them, just as he wanted them to be" (v. 18). "God" here certainly seems to refer to the Third Member of the Trinity, the Holy Spirit.

8. The sovereign assembling of the body by the Holy Spirit should not lead to division in the body but to an "equal concern for each other" (v. 25).

9. Again we are reminded that "God has placed in the church" certain people and gifts. "God" in verse 28 seems to refer to the Spirit of God. The people and gifts mentioned in verses 28-30 are: apostles, prophets; teachers; miracles; gifts of healing, helping, guidance; and of different kinds of tongues. [I find it interesting that three gifts — healing, helping, guidance — seem to be a small category of gifts].

10. Lastly, this same Spirit who disburses different gifts longs for unity among believers. Several questions are asked in verses 29-30 to show that there are different gifts among the people of God.

Let's take a brief look at our third passage — Ephesians 4 —

As a prisoner for the Lord, then, I urge you to live a life worthy of the calling you have received. [2] Be completely humble and gentle; be patient, bearing with one another in love. [3] Make every effort to keep the unity of the Spirit through the bond of peace. [4] There is one body and one Spirit, just as you were called to one hope when you were called; [5] one Lord, one faith, one baptism; [6] one God and Father of all, who is over all and through all and in all.

[7] But to each one of us grace has been given as Christ apportioned it. [8] This is why it says:

"When he ascended on high,
he took many captives
and gave gifts to his people."

[9] (What does "he ascended" mean except that he also descended to the lower, earthly regions? [10] He who descended is the very one who ascended higher than all the heavens, in order to fill the whole universe.) [11] So Christ himself gave the apostles, the prophets, the evangelists, the pastors and teachers, [12] to equip his people for works of service, so that the body of Christ may be built up [13] until we all reach unity in the faith

and in the knowledge of the Son of God and become mature, attaining to the whole measure of the fullness of Christ.

[14] Then we will no longer be infants, tossed back and forth by the waves, and blown here and there by every wind of teaching and by the cunning and craftiness of people in their deceitful scheming. [15] Instead, speaking the truth in love, we will grow to become in every respect the mature body of him who is the head, that is, Christ. [16] From him the whole body, joined and held together by every supporting ligament, grows and builds itself up in love, as each part does its work.

In this third passage on spiritual gifts, we see that the emphasis is on the "unity of the Spirit" (v. 3). Paul stresses the oneness of the body and of the Spirit and of "the hope when you were called, one Lord, one faith, one baptism, one God and Father of all, who is over all and through all and in all." (vv. 5-6).

We learn that Christ (through the Spirit) "gave gifts to his people" (v. 8). The gifts listed in this text are: the apostles, the prophets, the evangelists, the pastors and teachers (v. 11).

Why are these gifts given? We are clearly told they are given "to equip his people for works of service, so that the body of Christ may be built up" (v. 12). But building up the body also involves strengthening the body to no longer be infants in its beliefs (vv. 14-16).

Let's look at the last of our four passages, 1 Peter 4 —

[7] The end of all things is near. Therefore be alert and of sober mind so that you may pray. [8] Above all, love each other deeply, because love covers over a multitude of sins. [9] Offer hospitality to one another without grumbling. [10] Each of you should use whatever gift you have received to serve others, as faithful stewards of God's grace in its various forms. [11] If anyone speaks, they should do so as one who speaks the very words of God. If anyone serves, they should do so with the strength God provides, so that in all things God may be praised through Jesus Christ. To him be the glory and the power for ever and ever. Amen.

What do we learn here about God the Holy Spirit? Actually He is not specifically mentioned in this last text on spiritual gifts, but we may infer several truths:

1. We are told to "use whatever gift you have received to serve others" (v. 10). And we know from our other texts that the Spirit is the Giver of the gifts.

2. We are to be "faithful stewards of God's grace in its various forms" (v. 10). It is the Spirit of God who is the grace-giver, "grace" referring to the gifts themselves.

3. One question would be: Who is the "God" being referred to in verse 11?

We read,

> 11 If anyone speaks, they should do so as one who speaks the very words of God. If anyone serves, they should do so with the strength God provides, so that in all things God may be praised through Jesus Christ. To him be the glory and the power for ever and ever. Amen.

Could "God" in this verse be referring to the Third Member of the Trinity, the Holy Spirit? If so, the one who has the gift of speaking should do so as one "who speaks the very words of God" (the Holy Spirit). After all, it is the Spirit who led the Apostles to write the New Testament. Now, it does not appear that verse 11 is saying that new revelation is being given or that it should be added to the divine canon of Scripture.

Further, the one who serves should serve "with the strength God [the Holy Spirit?] provides." Why? "So that in all things God [the Holy Spirit?] may be praised through Jesus Christ." Could this be another reference to the Third Member of the Trinity? He is worthy to be praised and to receive "glory and power for ever and ever."

The Challenge: In all four of these texts on the spiritual gifts, it appears that much of the work which the Spirit of God is doing in the church and in the world is through God's gifted-people.

(4) THE FRUIT OF THE HOLY SPIRIT

In our Christian lives we are so often like the drunk cowboy who gets on his horse and falls off on the right side, promptly remounts and falls off on the left side. When it comes to God the Holy Spirit, some believers over**emphasize** Him while others over**look** Him. We want a balanced view of the Third Member of the Trinity.

We have suggested that because He is personal, we can speak to Him. And because He is divine, we can worship Him. Neither of these actions are at the expense of our first love, the Lord Jesus, the One the Spirit came to glorify.

The Holy Spirit is invisible, so how do we know that He is real and that He is working in our lives? While invisibility does not equal non-existence, the Spirit shows His presence by the works He does in and through believers. One of His primary works is to produce fruit in the Jesus-follower's life. We read in Galatians 5 —

> [16] So I say, walk by the Spirit, and you will not gratify the desires of the flesh. [17] For the flesh desires what is contrary to the Spirit, and the Spirit what is contrary to the flesh. They are in conflict with each other, so that you are not to do whatever[c] you want. [18] But if you are led by the Spirit, you are not under the law.
>
> [19] The acts of the flesh are obvious: sexual immorality, impurity and debauchery; [20] idolatry and witchcraft; hatred, discord, jealousy, fits of rage, selfish ambition, dissensions, factions [21] and envy; drunkenness, orgies, and the like. I warn you, as I did before, that those who live like this will not inherit the kingdom of God.
>
> [22] But the fruit of the Spirit is love, joy, peace, forbearance, kindness, goodness, faithfulness, [23] gentleness and self-control. Against such things there is no law. [24] Those who belong to Christ Jesus have crucified the flesh with its passions and desires. [25] Since we live by the Spirit, let us keep in step with the Spirit. [26] Let us not become conceited, provoking and envying each other.

In this section Paul is contrasting the Spirit and the flesh. "The flesh" here refers to our sinful nature which desires what is contrary to the Spirit. The Spirit is not uninvolved — He desires what is contrary to the flesh (v. 17). This conflict between the Spirit and the flesh is "fleshed out" in verses 19-26.

The "acts of the flesh" are obvious and are listed as the "Filthy Fifteen": sexual immorality, impurity, debauchery, idolatry, witchcraft, hatred, discord, jealousy, fits of rage, selfish ambition, dissensions, factions, envy, drunkenness, and orgies. And, as if that list isn't enough, Paul adds, "and the like" (v. 21). Notice that these "acts" have to do with sexual purity, who or what we worship, dabbling with the demonic, internal attitudes like hatred and jealousy, the improper use of our temper, self-centered living, loss of self-control, and a complete abandonment to immorality.

We then have an opposite list of **the fruit of the Spirit.** This list entails nine Spiritual Attitudes which inevitably manifest themselves in how we relate to others. The fruit include: love, joy, peace, forbearance, kindness, goodness, faithfulness, gentleness, and self-control.

Apart from helping us with our identity, the Third Person of the Godhead wishes to produce in us the fruit of the Spirit. Galatians 5:16-25 teaches us about the "desires of the sinful nature" (verse 16-21) and the fruit of the Spirit (verses 22-25). Paul reminds us that the development of love, joy, peace, patience, etc. is not "against the law"! You'll never get a ticket for being too loving. And you'll never be arrested for having too much self-control. In Ephesians 5:8-10 the believers are told that "You were once darkness, but now you are light in the Lord. Live as children of light (for the fruit of the light consists in all goodness, righteousness and truth) and find out what pleases the Lord."

The Challenge: Do you claim to be filled with the Spirit, led by Him? Check for fruit in your life!

(5) THE ILLUMINATION OF THE HOLY SPIRIT

"He *illumines* the believer? What in the world are you talking about?", you might say. We know that the Spirit of God was sent by Jesus as His substitute Teacher. We read the following in the Upper Room Discourse (John 14-16):

> [25] "All this I have spoken while still with you. [26] But the Advocate, the Holy Spirit, whom the Father will send in my name, will teach you all things and will remind you of everything I have said to you. (John 14)
>
> [26] "When the Advocate comes, whom I will send to you from the Father—the Spirit of truth who goes out from the Father—he will testify about me. (John 15)
>
> [12] "I have much more to say to you, more than you can now bear. [13] But when he, the Spirit of truth, comes, he will guide you into all the truth. He will not speak on his own; he will speak only what he hears, and he will tell you what is yet to come. [14] He will glorify me because it is from me that he will receive what he will make known to you. [15] All that belongs to the Father is mine. That is why I said the Spirit will receive from me what he will make known to you." (John 16)

We must make several points about these verses in John 14-16-

1. The Spirit of God will teach the disciples all things and will remind them of everything Jesus had said to them (John 14:26).

The primary application of this verse is to the original Apostles and seems to be a reference to their being taught and guided into writing the New Testament Scriptures.

A secondary application which seems valid is that this verse applies to all believers who pay attention to what the Lord Jesus said. They will receive the Spirit's help in focusing upon Christ's teachings.

2. The Spirit of God is "the Spirit of truth" and "will testify" about the Lord Jesus (John 15:26).

There is a definite curriculum for the Substitute Teacher and it is ... the Lord Jesus.

3. This "Spirit of truth" will "guide [the disciples] into all the truth" (John 16:12). His teaching ministry will not be a solo work — "He will speak only what He hears."

There is an order in the Trinity that no one, especially theologians, understands. But John 16 indicates that the Spirit's role is to "glorify" the Son. And the Spirit "will receive from [the Lord Jesus] what He will make known to you" (John 16:15).

So, what does this have to do with illumination? The Spirit of God is intimately involved in the believer's studying the words of the Lord Jesus, and, by extension, his or her diligent study of any of the written Word of God.

This personal relationship with the Holy Spirit is *in addition to* our relationship with the Lord Jesus. The Spirit comes to glorify Christ, not Himself. So Jesus should receive our primary attention. But "primary" does not mean "exclusive." As we examine the ministries of the Holy Spirit, let's think a bit more about His ministry of illumination.

We've seen from the Upper Room Discourse (John 14-16) that the Spirit of God was sent by Jesus as His substitute Teacher (14:26), that He is the "Spirit of truth" and "will testify" about the Lord Jesus (John 15:26). This means His primary curriculum is none other than the Lord Jesus Christ Himself! His teaching ministry will not be a solo work — "He will speak only what He hears." And we saw that the Spirit "will receive from [the Lord Jesus] what He will make known to you" (John 16:15).

We concluded that the Spirit of God is intimately involved in the believer's studying the words of the Lord Jesus, and, by extension, his or her diligent study of any of the written Word of God.

There is another key text about the Spirit's ministry of illumination and it is found in 1 Corinthians 2 where we read —

> [6] We do, however, speak a message of wisdom among the mature, but not the wisdom of this age or of the rulers of this age, who are coming to nothing. [7] No, we declare God's wisdom, a mystery that has been hidden and that God destined

for our glory before time began. [8] None of the rulers of this age understood it, for if they had, they would not have crucified the Lord of glory. [9] However, as it is written:

"What no eye has seen,
what no ear has heard,
and what no human mind has conceived"—
the things God has prepared for those who love him—
    [10] these are the things God has revealed to us by his Spirit.

    The Spirit searches all things, even the deep things of God. [11] For who knows a person's thoughts except their own spirit within them? In the same way no one knows the thoughts of God except the Spirit of God. [12] What we have received is not the spirit of the world, but the Spirit who is from God, so that we may understand what God has freely given us. [13] This is what we speak, not in words taught us by human wisdom but in words taught by the Spirit, explaining spiritual realities with Spirit-taught words. [14] The person without the Spirit does not accept the things that come from the Spirit of God but considers them foolishness, and cannot understand them because they are discerned only through the Spirit. [15] The person with the Spirit makes judgments about all things, but such a person is not subject to merely human judgments, [16] for,

    "Who has known the mind of the Lord
      so as to instruct him?"
    But we have the mind of Christ.

This is a difficult passage to understand. But what do we learn specifically here about the Spirit of God?

1. The Spirit reveals truths to us — truths that are not discovered by the wise of this world, a mystery none of the rulers of this age understood (vv. 6-8).

2. These truths surpass what the eye has seen and the ear has heard and the human mind is able to conceive. These are the things God has prepared for those who love Him. And these things have been revealed to us by His Spirit (vv. 9-10).

3. These "thoughts of God" are those which no one knows "except the Spirit of God" (v. 11). We have received this Spirit "so that we may understand what God has freely given us" (v. 12).

4. Our speaking these truths ought to be not with words of human wisdom but "in words taught by the Spirit, explaining spiritual realities with Spirit-taught words" (v. 13).

5. But what about the unsaved person? We are told that "The person without the Spirit does not accept the things that come from the Spirit of God but considers them foolishness, and cannot understand them because they are discerned only through the Spirit" (v. 14). There is a discernment that only the Spirit of God can give. And He gives that discernment only to those who "have" the Spirit.

The person without the Spirit does not "accept the things that come from the Spirit but considers them foolishness." The word "accept" is a verb that means to "warmly embrace."

Conclusion: The illuminating ministry of the Spirit of God involves His helping the believer warmly embrace the truths of God. It is not a substitute for the diligent study of the Word. It is not a substitute for proper principles of interpretation (hermeneutics). The Spirit of God *works with* the believer in not only understanding God's truth, but applying God's truth to himself and others.

(6) The Sealing of the Holy Spirit

One ministry of the Spirit I've heard virtually nothing about is His sealing ministry. Here are the primary passages on this work of the Spirit of God:

John 6:27
Do not work for food that spoils, but for food that endures to eternal life, which the Son of Man will give you. **For on him God the Father has placed his seal of approval."**

1 Corinthians 9:2
Even though I may not be an apostle to others, surely I

am to you! For **you are the seal of my apostleship in the Lord.**

2 Corinthians 1:21-22
[21] Now it is God who makes both us and you stand firm in Christ. He anointed us, [22] **set his seal of ownership on us**, and put his Spirit in our hearts as a deposit, guaranteeing what is to come.

Ephesians 1:13
And you also were included in Christ when you heard the message of truth, the gospel of your salvation. When you believed, **you were marked in him with a seal, the promised Holy Spirit,**

Ephesians 4:30
And do not grieve the Holy Spirit of God, **with whom you were sealed** for the day of redemption.

We learn from John 6 that God the Father placed His seal of approval on the Son of Man. Paul declares in 1 Corinthians 9 that the Corinthians "are the seal of my apostleship in the Lord."

We are told in 2 Corinthians 1 that God has "set his seal of ownership on us …" How has He done that? The passage goes on and says, "and put his Spirit in our hearts as a deposit, guaranteeing what is to come" (v. 22).

Ephesians 1 makes it clear that after we believed we "were marked in him with a seal, the promised Holy Spirit" (v. 13). Paul then tells us in chapter 4 that we are not to grieve the Holy Spirit of God, "with whom you were sealed for the day of redemption" (v. 30).

GotQuestions.org has the following helpful summary:
Question: "What is the seal of the Holy Spirit?"
Answer: The Holy Spirit is referred to as the "deposit," "seal," and "earnest" in the hearts of Christians (2 Corinthians 1:22; 5:5; Ephe-

sians 1:13-14; 4:30). The Holy Spirit is God's seal on His people, His claim on us as His very own. The Greek word translated "earnest" in these passages is *arrhabōn* which means "a pledge," that is, part of the purchase money or property given in advance as security for the rest. The gift of the Spirit to believers is a down payment on our heavenly inheritance, which Christ has promised us and secured for us at the cross. It is because the Spirit has sealed us that we are assured of our salvation. No one can break the seal of God.

The Holy Spirit is given to believers as a "first installment" to assure us that our full inheritance as children of God will be delivered. The Holy Spirit is given to us to confirm to us that we belong to God who grants to us His Spirit as a gift, just as grace and faith are gifts (Ephesians 2:8-9). Through the gift of the Spirit, God renews and sanctifies us. He produces in our hearts those feelings, hopes, and desires which are evidence that we are accepted by God, that we are regarded as His adopted children, that our hope is genuine, and that our redemption and salvation are sure in the same way that a seal guarantees a will or an agreement. God grants to us His Holy Spirit as the certain pledge that we are His forever and shall be saved in the last day. The proof of the Spirit's presence is His operations on the heart which produce repentance, the fruit of the Spirit (Galatians 5:22-23), conformity to God's commands and will, a passion for prayer and praise, and love for His people. These things are the evidences that the Holy Spirit has renewed the heart and that the Christian is sealed for the day of redemption.

So it is through the Holy Spirit and His teachings and guiding power that we are sealed and confirmed until the day of redemption, complete and free from the corruption of sin and the grave. Because we have the seal of the Spirit in our hearts, we can live joyfully, confident of our sure place in a future that holds unimaginable glories.[8]

---

8   https://www.gotquestions.org/Holy-Spirit-seal.html

STUDY QUESTIONS:

1. How do we best cooperate with the teaching ministry of the Spirit of God?

2. Are we to pray for the filling of the Holy Spirit? Write out a sample prayer of your praying for His filling.

3. What gift or gifts has the Holy Spirit given you? How do you know?

4. What specific fruit of the Spirit are you working on right now in your life?

5. How is the truth of the Spirit's sealing ministry a comfort to you?

CHAPTER 6

HIS MINISTRIES TO THE BELIEVER (PART 3)

"Write down the date of the last known sin you confessed," I said to the mid-week church service attendees. "Don't specify the sin — and don't put your name on your card." I read some of the cards out loud. One wrote, "My last known sin that I confessed was in 1958 when I trusted Christ as my Savior." Another said, "Twenty years ago I confessed my anger when my wife ran off with the vacuum cleaner salesman." "Really?", I said to the congregation, as I started to preach my message on the ministries of God the Holy Spirit.

(1) THE CONVICTING OF THE BELIEVER BY THE HOLY SPIRIT

What in the world convinces Christians that the Holy Spirit only convicts the world of their sin? What about us? What about the many areas in which we need His divine finger to point out to us our bad thinking, poor choices, and misguided priorities?

But how does God the Holy Spirit bring about conviction of sin in the believer's life? Again, if His primary tool is the Word of God, then the Word properly preached (or shared) is the vehicle by which the Holy Spirit brings biblical guilt into the heart of the Christian. There is, of course, unbiblical guilt which the world (and even other Christians) tries to inflict upon us. But biblical guilt occurs when the Holy Spirit gets real specific with us about something that needs to change — and we submit to His leading.

Some of you know that I did my doctoral dissertation on the doctrine of the Holy Spirit. After reading 55 volumes of tough theological material, one particular truth stood out to me about the Holy Spirit and the conviction of sin. Darby said that conviction of sin occurs when I stop defending myself and go and stand with the Holy Spirit in condemning the sin in my life. I thought that was helpful.

Where has the Holy Spirit brought a kind of biblical guilt to your soul? Are you standing with Him and asking God to help you abandon that sin, change that habit, repent of that attitude?

(2) THE HOLY SPIRIT'S HELP IN OUR PRAYER LIFE

Romans 8 is the classic passage on much of what the Holy Spirit wants to do in the believer's life. Let's notice that text carefully:

> [22] We know that the whole creation has been groaning as in the pains of childbirth right up to the present time. [23] Not only so, but we ourselves, who have the firstfruits of the Spirit, groan inwardly as we wait eagerly for our adoption to sonship, the redemption of our bodies. [24] For in this hope we were saved. But hope that is seen is no hope at all. Who hopes for what they already have? [25] But if we hope for what we do not yet have, we wait for it patiently.
>
> [26] In the same way, the Spirit helps us in our weakness. We do not know what we ought to pray for, but the Spirit himself intercedes for us through wordless groans. [27] And he who searches our hearts knows the mind of the Spirit, because the Spirit intercedes for God's people in accordance with the will of God.
>
> [28] And we know that in all things God works for the good of those who love him, who[i] have been called according to his purpose. [29] For those God foreknew he also predestined to be conformed to the image of his Son, that he might be the firstborn among many brothers and sisters. [30] And those he predestined, he also called; those he called, he also justified; those he justified, he also glorified. (Romans 8)

How does the Holy Spirit assist us in our prayer lives? Several specific points come from Romans 8:

(1) The Spirit is sensitive to our fallen condition. The whole creation is groaning in its brokenness; we are eagerly waiting for our adoption to sonship, and we long for our glorified bodies like our Lord Jesus (vv. 22-23).

(2) The Spirit helps us in our weakness. He somehow assists us in our ignorance about what we should pray for (v. 26). And He intercedes for us "through wordless groans" (v. 26). There is a profound mystery here, but we must believe that the Holy Spirit is active in interceding for the people of God according to the will of God (v. 27).

(3) We can be confident of His help in conforming us to the image of His Son (vv. 28-30).

I do not need to depend upon my oral skills for the Lord to hear my prayers. The Holy Spirit is intimately involved in what concerns me and He helps shape and conform my desires to what they ought to be. And, somehow, mysteriously, He is involved in my pouring out my heart to the Lord.

(3) THE LEADING OF THE HOLY SPIRIT

The next ministry of God the Holy Spirit that we want to consider is His leading. If He is indeed personal, He can lead the people of God. But, we must ask, what saith the Scriptures?

Matthew 4:1— [Jesus Is Tested in the Wilderness] Then Jesus was **led by the Spirit** into the wilderness to be tempted by the devil.

Acts 13 — [1] Now in the church at Antioch there were prophets and teachers: Barnabas, Simeon called Niger, Lucius of Cyrene, Manaen (who had been brought up with Herod the tetrarch) and Saul. [2] While they were worshiping the Lord and fasting, the Holy Spirit said, **"Set apart for me Barnabas and**

Saul for the work to which I have called them." [3] So after
they had fasted and prayed, they placed their hands on them
and sent them off.

Romans 8:14 — For those who are **led by the Spirit of
God** are the children of God.

Galatians 5:18 — But if you are **led by the Spirit,** you
are not under the law.

How does God the Holy Spirit lead His people? God has
certainly used dreams and visions in the Word of God to move
His children in certain directions (one thinks of the Apostle Peter
in Acts 10). Should we strive for and long for dreams and visions
today? If we do, it seems that we are minimizing the Word of God
and the Spirit's leading the people of God … through the people of
God! What I mean is, isn't it the case that most of what the Spirit
does today He does *mediately*? By "mediately" we mean through
human instruments. He does not appear to perform His ministries
today primarily *immediately* (not as to time, but as to directness).

The idea of "finding the will of God," by the way, is not a
magical quest that only a few Christians are able to successfully
complete. In fact, Dr. Bruce Waltke (in his excellent book *Finding
the Will of God: A Pagan Notion?*) rightly suggests that some forms
of "seeking God's will" smack more of divination than devotion.
How does God lead you? Isn't it through a face-to-face encounter
with God's truth in God's Word? Isn't it through a believer who
loves you enough to tell you the truth about something hard? Isn't
it in the quietness of your soul when you pray and ask God to move
your heart to seek Him more deeply?

(4) THE ASSURANCE OF THE HOLY SPIRIT

Let's consider the internal ministry of assurance which the
Spirit of God gives the believer. We read in Romans 8 —

> [14] For those who are led by the Spirit of God are the
> children of God. [15] The Spirit you received does not make
> you slaves, so that you live in fear again; rather, the Spirit you

received brought about your adoption to sonship. And by him we cry, *"Abba,* Father." [16] The Spirit himself testifies with our spirit that we are God's children. [17] Now if we are children, then we are heirs—heirs of God and co-heirs with Christ, if indeed we share in his sufferings in order that we may also share in his glory.

What we see in these incredible verses from Romans 8 ought to bring encouragement to the believer's heart. It is by the Spirit that we cry, "Abba, Father" (v. 15).

What about when you've really blown it as a believer and you think, "There's no way that God loves me right now or calls me His child!"? We read in verse 16- "The Spirit Himself testifies with our spirit that we are God's children."

God the Holy Spirit assures us that we are His children. And not only that, but we are heirs — "heirs of God and co-heirs with Christ" (v. 17). The biblical doctrine of assurance is one ministry of the Spirit of God to our hearts — and it ought to calm our hearts and steady our minds in living for Him!

STUDY QUESTIONS:

1. What is the Spirit's primary tool in bringing conviction to the believer's heart?

2. How exactly does the Spirit help us in our prayer lives?

3. What are some dangers in our asking the Spirit of God to "lead" us?

4. How does the Spirit's ministry of assurance differ from the sin of presumption?

CHAPTER 7

HIS MINISTRIES TO THE UNBELIEVER

"I have a lot of unsaved friends," Bill said to me. "I know I'm to live my life before them, but how does the Holy Spirit fit in the process? What does He do?" "I'm so glad you asked!", I said.

THE UNBELIEVER AND THE HOLY SPIRIT

What are the ministries of the Spirit of God to the unbeliever? Scripture is clear that His primary ministry is that of conviction of sin. We read in John 16:

When he [the Spirit of God] comes, he will convict the world of guilt in regard to sin and righteousness and judgment: in regard to sin, because men do not believe in me; in regard to righteousness, because I am going to the Father, where you can see me no longer; and in regard to judgment, because the prince of this world now stands condemned. (verses 8-11)

The Spirit's inner ministry of convicting the unbeliever of sin is mysterious, but we need to pray for His work in the hearts of family members, co-workers, and acquaintances who have not yet received the gospel. I believe that we need to ask God the Holy Spirit to grant repentance to those we love who are outside of Christ. That expression — "grant repentance" — is used twice in God's Word. In Acts 11 we read of the early church that they praised God who had "granted repentance" to the Gentiles, a repentance that "leads to life" (v. 18). The second use of this expression occurs in 2 Timothy where Paul gives Timothy advice about his theological opponents.

Paul writes, "Opponents must be gently instructed, in the hope that God will grant them repentance leading them to a knowledge of the truth …" (2 Timothy 2:25).

I have often been impressed as I have read through the book of Acts (especially Acts 16:14) by the co-operation between the Apostles' preaching the gospel convincingly and the Spirit of God bringing conviction. Perhaps if we did our job more conscientiously, He would do His work more frequently.

A second ministry of the Spirit of God to unbelievers is that of restraining sin in the world. This work of the Holy Spirit seems to be implied in 2 Thessalonians 2:7 where we read, "For the secret power of lawlessness is already at work; but the one who now holds it back will continue to do so till he is taken out of the way." Although some commentators think this verse is referring to the savoring effect of the church, others suggest it is the Spirit of God who is holding back or restricting or controlling sin in the world (see also Genesis 6:3 concerning the Spirit's "striving" with man). Every generation of Christians seems to think its own to be the most sinful in history. How easily we can forget this divine work of the Spirit in our lost world.

STUDY QUESTIONS:

1. How might we work with the Holy Spirit in His ministry of convicting our unsaved friends of their need of Christ?

2. Would you agree with the statement that our job is convincing the unbeliever of the truth of the gospel and the Holy Spirit's job is convicting the unbeliever of his or her sin and need of Christ? How does the book of Acts help answer this question?

3. What are some ways that the Holy Spirit restrains sin in the world?

CHAPTER 8

OUR RESPONSE TO THE SPIRIT OF GOD

"Okay. Okay!", my friend Alice said. "I'm convinced that I need to become more aware of the Spirit's ministries in my life, that in that sense I can develop a 'relationship' with Him. I want to worship Him as God and cooperate with what He is seeking to do in and through my life. But let's get specific. How am I to treat God the Holy Spirit?" "I'm so glad you asked," I responded.

We want to conclude our study by asking a number of questions: What does it mean to "quench" the Spirit? In what ways do we "grieve" the Holy Spirit? How in the world are we to "pray in the Spirit"?

THE QUENCHING OF THE SPIRIT

We read in 1 Thessalonians 5:19 — "Do not quench the Spirit." (NIV) Other translations of this verse put it a bit differently: The NET Bible has "Do not extinguish the Spirit." The Living Bible says, "Do not smother the Holy Spirit." The CSB renders this verse as: "Don't stifle the Spirit." The CEB says, "Don't suppress the Spirit" while the ICB has "Do not stop the work of the Holy Spirit."

So, we are not to extinguish or smother the Holy Spirit. We can somehow stifle Him or suppress Him, stopping His work in and through us. The context of 1 Thessalonians 5:19 mentions prophesying and the Phillips' translation renders the text as: "Never damp the fire of the Spirit, and never despise what is spoken in the name of the Lord. By all means use your judgement, and hold on to whatever is really good, Steer clear of evil in any form." *The Message* says: "Don't suppress the Spirit, and don't stifle those who have a word from the Master. On the other hand, don't be gullible. Check out everything, and keep only what's good. Throw out anything tainted with evil."

So — what does it mean to quench the Spirit of God? One writer helps us understand this particular issue. When the word "quench" is used in Scripture, it is speaking of suppressing fire. When believers put on the shield of faith, as part of their armor of God (Ephesians 6:16), they are extinguishing the power of the fiery darts from Satan. Christ described hell as a place where the fire would not be "quenched" (Mark 9:44, 46, 48). Likewise, the Holy Spirit is a fire dwelling in each believer. He wants to express Himself in our actions and attitudes. When believers do not allow the Spirit to be seen in our actions, when we do what we know is wrong, we suppress or quench the Spirit (1 Thessalonians 5:19). We do not allow the Spirit to reveal Himself the way that He wants to.[9]

The Challenge: How might you be quenching the Spirit of God's fire in your life? Confess that — and ask Him to continue His good work in you.

Here's a bonus summary of an article on this issue:

"SEVEN WAYS WE QUENCH THE HOLY SPIRIT" (SAM STORMS)

1. We quench the Holy Spirit when we rely decisively on any resource other than the Holy Spirit for anything we do in life and ministry.
2. We quench the Spirit whenever we diminish his personality and speak of him as if he were only an abstract power or source of divine energy.

---

9   https://www.gotquestions.org/grieve-quench-Holy-Spirit.html

3. We quench the Spirit whenever we suppress or legislate against his work of imparting spiritual gifts and ministering to the church through them.

4. We quench the Spirit whenever we create an inviolable and sanctimonious structure in our corporate gatherings and worship services, and in our small groups, that does not permit spontaneity or the special leading of the Spirit.

5. We quench the Spirit whenever we despise prophetic utterances (1 Thessalonians 5:20).

6. We quench the Spirit whenever we diminish his activity that alerts and awakens us to the glorious and majestic truth that we are truly the children of God (Romans 8:15–16; Galatians 4:4–7).

7. We quench the Spirit whenever we suppress, or legislate against, or instill fear in the hearts of people regarding the legitimate experience of heartfelt emotions and affections in worship.[10]

THE GRIEVING OF THE SPIRIT OF GOD

One of my seminary students wrote a paper on "The Lost Art of Lament." She made the case that we have virtually forgotten how to grieve over our sins. Isn't it true that our prayers are often skeleton supplications for God to bless us? When we worship or adore God in prayer, have we skipped lament? We ought to *grieve* over our sins to be sure. But do we ever *grieve* the Spirit of God?

We are not to grieve the Spirit of God. We read in Ephesians 4:30 —

> And do not grieve the Holy Spirit of God, with whom you were sealed for the day of redemption.

There are quite a few verses in the Bible about grieving.

Genesis 6:5-6- 5 And God saw that the wickedness of man was great in the earth, and that every imagination of the thoughts of his

10 https://www.desiringgod.org/articles/seven-ways-to-quench-the-spirit

heart was only evil continually. 6 And it repented the Lord that he had made man on the earth, and **it grieved him at his hear**t. (KJV)

Genesis 18:20 Then the Lord said, "The outcry against Sodom and Gomorrah is so great and their sin **so grievous …**

Deuteronomy 34:8 The Israelites **grieved** for Moses in the plains of Moab thirty days, until the time of weeping and mourning was over.

1 Samuel 20:34 Jonathan got up from the table in fierce anger; on that second day of the feast he did not eat, because he was **grieved** at his father's shameful treatment of David.

2 Samuel 1:26 I **grieve** for you, Jonathan my brother; you were very dear to me. Your love for me was wonderful, more wonderful than that of women.

Job 30:25 Have I not wept for those in trouble? Has not my soul **grieved** for the poor?

Psalm 78:40 How often they rebelled against him in the wilderness and **grieved him** in the wasteland!

Isaiah 63:10 Yet they rebelled and **grieved his Holy Spirit.** So he turned and became their enemy and he himself fought against them.

John 16:20 Very truly I tell you, you will weep and mourn while the world rejoices. You will **grieve**, but your grief will turn to joy.

Colossians 3:13 Bear with each other and forgive one another if any of you has a **grievance** against someone. Forgive as the Lord forgave you.

1 Thessalonians 4:13 Brothers and sisters, we do not want you to be uninformed about those who sleep in death, so that you do not **grieve** like the rest of mankind, who have no hope.

Here are several observations about grief and grieving in the Scriptures:

1. God grieves! God is "grieved at his heart" that he had made man (Gen. 6:6).

2. God grieves at the wickedness of Sodom and Gomorrah ("their sin so grievous") (Genesis 18:20).

3. People grieve for other people in the Bible (the Israelites for Moses [Deuteronomy 34:8], Jonathan's grief at his father's shameful treatment of David [1 Samuel 20:34], David's grief at Jonathan's death [2 Samuel 1:26], etc.).

4. Job defends himself as grieving for the poor and weeping for those in trouble (Job 30:25).

5. We are told very specifically that Israel rebelled against God and "grieved him in the wasteland" (Psalm 78:40).

6. In the Old Testament we learn that the Israelites "rebelled and grieved his Holy Spirit. So he turned and became their enemy and he himself fought against them" (Isaiah 63:10).

7. We are to forgive others whatever grievance we have against them (Colossians 3:13).

8. Jesus says that there will be both weeping and rejoicing: "Very truly I tell you, you will weep and mourn while the world rejoices. You will grieve, but your grief will turn to joy" (John 16:20).

9. Lastly, we are to grieve at the death of those we love, but we are told, "you do not grieve like the rest of mankind, who have no hope" (1 Thessalonians 4:13).

Conclusion: We can — and often do — grieve God the Holy Spirit. Grieving our and another's sin is right and good. But we must recognize that because He is a Person, the Spirit of God can be grieved by our unbelief and rebellion. May I ask: Is there anything you need to apologize to the Holy Spirit for?

If we can grieve the Spirit, does it not make sense that we can bring Him joy?

PRAYING IN THE SPIRIT

We have a fascinating command in the one-chapter epistle of Jude where he writes,

But you, dear friends, by building yourselves up **in** your most holy faith and **praying in the Holy Spirit** … (Jude 1:20)

What in the world does it mean to "pray in the Holy Spirit"? This expression is used only one other time in Scripture and that is in Ephesians 6:18 where we read,

And **pray in the Spirit** on all occasions with all kinds of prayers and requests. With this in mind, be alert and always keep on praying for all the Lord's people.

Does "praying in the Spirit" refer to the use of some supernatural, unlearned language? Some in the charismatic movement refer to "heavenly babbling," the speaking "in other tongues." However, when we examine the speaking in tongues on the Day of Pentecost, the disciples spoke in known dialects so that the gospel could be understood by people from various backgrounds.

There is nothing in the context of Jude 1 or of Ephesians 6 that would indicate that other-worldly languages are being referred to by the expression "praying in the Holy Spirit" or "pray in the Spirit." May I suggest a rather mundane, but hopefully accurate, view of this practice, and that would be — *We should pray in accordance with the Spirit's ministries.* In other words, in Jude the challenge is to stand strong for the gospel. To build ourselves up in our most holy faith involves praying that the Holy Spirit would have His way in our lives, that we would listen to His promptings, that we would obey His teaching of God's truth. In Ephesians our praying in the Spirit concerns others — We are to pray "in the Spirit" on all occasions with all kinds of prayers and requests. This involves being alert and consistent in praying for all the Lord's people.

Conclusion: We pray in the Spirit when we are aware of His works in our lives and we ask His help in doing our work for God. The self-work we do is to strengthen ourselves in God's truth. The others-work we do is to intercede for God's people.

The Challenge: Are you praying in the Holy Spirit? Take one of His ministries to you and ask Him to help you co-operate with His work in your life!

STUDY QUESTIONS:

1. What does it mean to "quench" the Spirit of God? In what ways might a believer do that?

2. Is there a place for the Christian to *apologize* to God the Holy Spirit for grieving Him? Write out a sample prayer of such an apology.

3. How do we practically "pray in the Holy Spirit"? What clues do we have from the epistle of Jude on this question?

CONCLUSION

We have tried to make the case in this book that the Holy Spirit, the Third Member of the Trinity, deserves our serious attention. Because He is personal, we can pray to Him and treat Him as One possessing intellect, emotions, and will. Because He is divine, it is good and proper for us to worship Him, praising Him for the many ministries He does in and for the believer.

While the Lord Jesus deserves our primary attention — and it is the Spirit's first mission to direct our attention to the Son of God — this does not mean that the Spirit should not receive the praise He is due. The thesis of this book is that we should desire a biblically-balanced view of the Third Person of the Trinity, the Holy Spirit of God. Some Christians overemphasize Him; others seem to overlook Him.

We were convicted by A.W. Tozer's charge when he said, "Our blunder (or shall we frankly say our sin?) has been to neglect the doctrine of the Spirit to a point where we virtually deny Him His place in the Godhead.... The doctrine of the Holy Spirit as held by evangelical Christians today has almost no practical value at all."

We pay the Spirit due respect when we understand His personality and His deity and when we appreciate His various ministries to believers and unbelievers alike. Although there is no biblical command to do so, I suggested that every believer should develop a kind of "relationship" with the Holy Spirit. By that term we mean understanding and cooperating with His work in the world and in us.

It is right and natural to pray to the Holy Spirit. Here are a few examples of such prayers that have helped me:

(1) "Holy Spirit, please guide me as I study the Word of God. Help me to warmly embrace what it says and protect me when I share it with others."

(2) "Dear Holy Spirit, please bring conviction of sin to my friend ___. He needs the Lord Jesus as his Savior. Help me do my best in answering whatever questions he has about the gospel. But I pray for Your internal work on his heart."

(3) "Divine Spirit of God, please forgive me for grieving You when I did ___. I want to please You by my life."

(4) "Spirit of God, I need Your internal assurance in my heart that You are with me and that I am loved as a child of God."

The Lord Jesus gives us much information about the Holy Spirit in the Upper Room Discourse (John 14-16). He makes it clear that the Holy Spirit cannot come unless the Son goes back to the Father. In that sense, this is the dispensation of the Spirit. But His primary role is to direct our attention, not to Himself, but to the Son of God.

If I treat the Holy Spirit as he deserves, I will use the gifts He has given me to build up the Body of Christ, allow Him to help me develop the fruit of the Spirit in my life, and give me a longing to do God's work, not in my own strength, but filled with His.

I will not misunderstand His role as "the other Comforter" in a way which allows me to become callous to the lostness around me. I will understand that He wants to give me strength (com-fort) to do the will of God.

I will never seek to divide the Spirit of God from the Word of God, for the Bible is His primary tool in making my life more like Christ's. And I will take full advantage of the Spirit's convicting ministry as I seek to convince my unbelieving friends of the truth of the gospel.

I will covenant not to grieve the Spirit or quench His fire in my life. And my practice of prayer will reflect His presence as my intercessor before the throne.